OFF BASE

Riddles about Baseball

by Rick & Ann Walton
pictures by Susan Slattery Burke

L Lerner Publications Company · Minneapolis

To Richard Ivie, who'll always go to bat for you   –R.W. & A.W.

To my wonderful daughter, Perrin, for her inspiration in this first year of her life   –S.S.B.

This book is available in two editions:
Library binding by Lerner Publications Company
Soft cover by First Avenue Editions
241 First Avenue North
Minneapolis, MN 55401

Library of Congress Cataloging-in-Publication Data

Walton, Rick.
  Off base : riddles about baseball / by Rick & Ann Walton ;
pictures by Susan Slattery Burke.
     p.   cm. – (You must be joking)
  Summary: A collection of riddles about baseball, including "Why
did the baseball coach buy a big broom? Because he wanted to sweep
the World Series."
  ISBN 0-8225-2338-8 (lib. bdg.)
  ISBN 0-8225-9639-3 (pbk.)
  1. Riddles, Juvenile. 2. Baseball–Juvenile humor. [1. Riddles.
2. Jokes. 3. Baseball–Wit and humor.] I. Walton, Ann, 1963-
II. Burke, Susan Slattery, ill. III. Title. IV. Series.
PN6371.5.W357 1993
818'.5402–dc20   92-19857
                                       CIP
                                       AC

Manufactured in the United States of America

1 2 3 4 5 6 98 97 96 95 94 93

Q: Who are the coolest dressers in baseball?

A: The Boston Rad Sox.

Q: Why did the baseball player take a mitt to the beach?

A: To catch some rays.

Q: When did the Sun play baseball?
A: In the All-Star game.

Q: What sport do thunderclouds like best?
A: Major Leak Baseball.

Q: What did the batter sing when the storm broke?
A: "I'm Swingin' in the Rain..."

Q: Who can start a fire by rubbing two baseball bats together?

A: A baseball scout.

Q: If a baseball field floods, how do the players get around?

A: In dugout canoes.

Q: Which baseball players trot around the bases?

A: The Philadelphia Fillies.

Q: What do the Philadelphia Fillies eat?

A: The Oakland Hays.

Q: Why is a batter like a horse's tail?

A: They're both fly swatters.

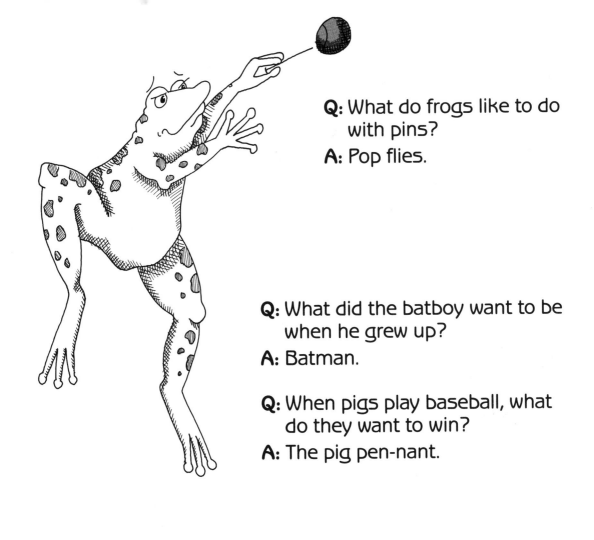

Q: What do frogs like to do
with pins?

A: Pop flies.

Q: What did the batboy want to be
when he grew up?

A: Batman.

Q: When pigs play baseball, what
do they want to win?

A: The pig pen-nant.

Q: What sport do honeybees play?
A: Beesball.

Q: What's colorful, light, and floats gracefully over a baseball field?
A: A batterfly.

Q: Where do batterflies come from?
A: Batterpillars.

Q: Why did Dracula go to the baseball game?

A: So he could play with the bats.

Q: How are three balls and two strikes like Dracula after dinner?

A: They're both full counts.

Q: Which baseball players put curses on their opponents?

A: The Montreal Hex-pos.

Q: What do baseball players do on Halloween?

A: They practice pitchcraft.

Q: Which baseball players will bite you if you try to run around the bases?

A: The New York Mutts.

Q: Why do batters spend a lot of time at playgrounds?

A: Because they like to swing.

Q: Why did the base runner feel like garbage?
A: Because he got thrown out.

Q: Where are the most outs made in baseball?
A: In the outfield.

Q: Why didn't the baseball club hire a janitor?
A: Because they already had a good cleanup hitter.

Q: Who plays baseball in your living room?
A: The home team.

Q: Who turns the lights on and off at the ballpark?

A: The switch-hitter.

Q: What's the difference between a bat and a battery?

A: One can make the hit, the other can make the heat.

Q: What do the Oakland A's hit with?

A: Alpha-bats.

Q: What kind of dishes do baseball players have?

A: Home plates.

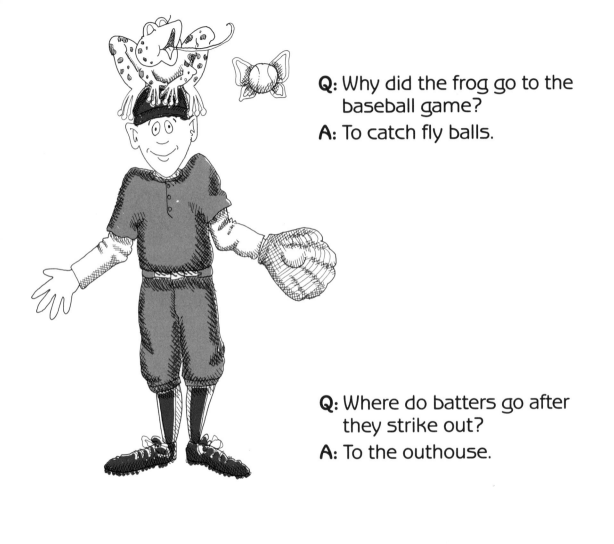

Q: Why did the frog go to the baseball game?

A: To catch fly balls.

Q: Where do batters go after they strike out?

A: To the outhouse.

Q: Why did the pitcher decide to become a matador instead?

A: Because he had spent so many years in the bullpen.

Q: Why did the baseball player practice milking cows?

A: Because he heard he was being sent to a farm team.

Q: Why won't the army draft baseball players?

A: Because the players might steal the bases.

Q: What do you become if you get caught stealing a base?

A: An out-law.

Q: What's the difference between a good pitcher and a prison warden?

A: One shuts people out, the other shuts people in.

Q: What's the difference between a fast base runner and a jewel thief?

A: One steals one base at a time, the other steals the whole diamond.

Q: What do you call a baseball player who throws a tantrum?

A: A baseball brat.

Q: Why are the longest sports articles about pitchers?

A: Because a pitcher's worth a thousand words.

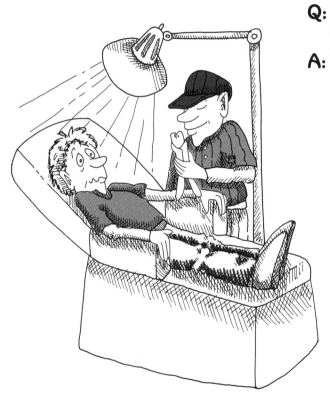

Q: Which baseball players want to be dentists?

A: The New York Yankers.

Q: What sport do astronauts play?

A: Spaceball.

Q: Who is the meanest person in baseball?
A: The pinch hitter.

Q: Why are baseballs white?
A: Because they keep getting hit into the bleachers.

Q: What baseball team is missing three players?
A: The Boston Red Six.

Q: What's red and white and black all over?
A: The Red Sox playing the White Sox at night.

Q: Why do baseball coaches go to art museums?

A: To look for good pitchers.

Q: What do pitchers sign their contracts with?

A: Bull pens.

Q: Why did the baseball coach buy a big broom?

A: Because he wanted to sweep the World Series.

Q: Why does the umpire brush off home plate?

A: It's his homework.

Q: What's the most common batting order?

A: "Batter up!"

Q: When dogs play baseball, who chases wild pitches?

A: The catcher's mutt.

Q: Why can't good catchers get away with anything?

A: Because they always get what's coming to them.

Q: Why did the batboy suddenly leave the baseball game?

A: He had to go to the batroom.

Q: Why did the baseball commissioner fine the fourth grader one thousand dollars?

A: For throwing spitballs in class.

Q: Why do baseball fans wear casual clothing?

A: Because ties aren't allowed in baseball.

Q: Why didn't the runner get to second base?

A: Because he was single-minded.

Q: Why did the baseball player cry when he reached home plate?

A: Because he missed third base.

Q: How would you feel if you ate home plate?

A: Homesick.

Q: When is a baseball game most explosive?

A: When the bases are loaded.

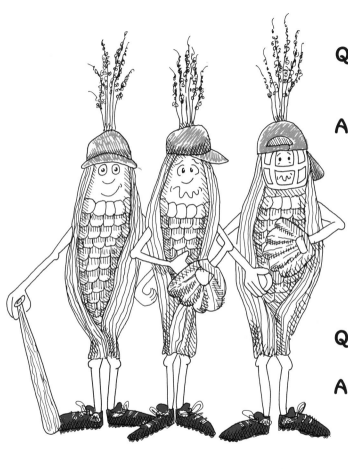

Q: Which baseball players repeat everything you say?

A: The Pittsburgh Parrots.

Q: Who are the corniest baseball players?

A: The Chicago Cobs.

Q: Why did the baseball player bring his car to the baseball game?

A: Because he wanted to drive in a run.

Q: Which baseball players always drive in runs?
A: The Chicago Cabs.

Q: Why did the batter get seasick?
A: Because he was on deck.

Q: How did the baseball player die?
A: He choked up on the bat.

Q: Where do baseball players clean their bats?
A: In the bat-tub.

Q: What did the girl do after she hit a baseball through her neighbor's window?
A: She made a home run.

ABOUT THE AUTHORS

Rick and Ann Walton love to read, travel, play guitar, take walks, study foreign languages, and write for children. Rick also collects books and writes music, and Ann knits and does origami. They live in Provo, Utah, where Ann is a computer programmer and Rick chases bats through the night sky. They have two spectacular children.

ABOUT THE ARTIST

Susan Slattery Burke loves to illustrate fun-loving characters, especially animals. To her, each of her characters has a personality all its own. She is most satisfied when the characters come to life for the reader as well. Susan lives in Minnetonka, Minnesota, with her husband, two daughters, and their dog and cat. Susan enjoys sculpting, reading, traveling, illustrating, and chasing her children around.

You Must Be Joking

Alphabatty: Riddles from A to Z
Help Wanted: Riddles about Jobs
Here's to Ewe: Riddles about Sheep
Hide and Shriek: Riddles about Ghosts and Goblins
Ho Ho Ho! Riddles about Santa Claus
Hoop-La: Riddles about Basketball
I Toad You So: Riddles about Frogs and Toads
Off Base: Riddles about Baseball
On with the Show: Show Me Riddles
Out on a Limb: Riddles about Trees and Plants
Take a Hike: Riddles about Football
That's for Shore: Riddles from the Beach
Weather or Not: Riddles for Rain and Shine
What's Gnu? Riddles from the Zoo
Wing It! Riddles about Birds